growing pains

mahika ray goswami

to everyone who's stuck in between

author's note

growing pains moves through the slow, shifting seasons of growth, capturing every ache and restless moment that shapes who we become. Across its four stages (inertia, displacement, resonance, and momentum) the collection follows the arc of change: stillness giving way to movement and silence giving way to voice.

Some pieces are rooted in traditions that have long carried stories of transformation. *quiet chaos* borrows from the cyclical rhythm and refrain of the West African epic *Gassire's Lute*, where each repetition marks both loss and progress. Its structure mirrors the cycle of returning and trying again, showing how persistence reshapes us. *homage to my silence* speaks in the bold, declarative style of Lucille Clifton's *homage to my hips*, reimagining silence as a force that commands space, protects, and endures.

This book is a conversation between who we are, who we've been, and who we hope to become. Like the dull aches we feel in our bones as we grow, the emotional shifts of becoming ourselves can be disorienting and necessary all at once. I wrote these poems to map those in-between spaces, where change feels both uncomfortable and inevitable. I hope that they soften the edges of your growing pains.

contents

contents

Part I: Inertia

Change doesn't always begin with movement. Sometimes it begins with stillness, like the quiet resistance slowly preparing for what comes next. Inertia is the resistance to change; it holds the weight of nostalgia and the urge to stay in the past because it's familiar, even when it no longer fits. It is the pause before the shift and a longing to remain untouched by time.

paint a pretty picture

let me paint you a pretty picture
of a kind of change unasked for
a kind of assumption blooming
that called for erasure and forgetfulness.

like the leaves fall in autumn
so too fell each of my fingers one by one
from my hopeful (hopeless) clutch
onto everything i knew
which was both a phone call
and a lifetime away.

i was in a city that i had only seen before
in a snowglobe
and i wished i could shake it up and make it disappear
i'd have shaken it forever
not letting the snow settle
until the glass cracked
so that i could finally crawl out
and get a taste of home again.

let me paint you a pretty picture.

letting things go

my room has been the same
since i was nine years old
and every picture on my wall holds a residual longing,
an echo of an unearthed fear
of letting things go
everybody can move onto better things,
it seems
but i stay shackled
within my room
a prisoner of an unwanted time capsule
since accepting this city means to let go of so much, and
letting go means forgetting home.

letting
go
means
forgetting
home.

so i hold onto the past
and keep my pictures as my only reprieve
but even those last memories
that i have desperately clung to,
those memories have already started to fade.

give me an inch and i'll make an archive

when i turned twelve, my best friend gifted me a candle.
its smell was sweet
and something i would have loved to fill my room with,
but i put it on my shelf next to my other unlit candles
and let it gather dust for years.

maybe i told myself i was saving it for later,
or maybe i just couldn't bring myself to use it at all.

if you were to ask me what i wanted for my birthday, i'd always say *i don't know*.
the point of a present is for it to mean something to the one who gets it,
but what i wanted was something that means a lot to the gift giver.
what i mean is
anything you give me will be worth as much as the fact that it was you
who gave it to me.

it was never about the candle.
i didn't burn it because i was afraid i'd be burning you with it.
but because i didn't
i still have that present from you from five years ago,
and even though we don't talk anymore, i have a part of you with me.

i admit, i'm a hoarder.
i hoard things to keep the people
who gave them to me closer than they are.

now i'm stuck with a row of unlit candles on my shelf
and i'll let the candles sit
gathering dust
because i can't bear to watch them burn.

time gone, now tinted

pink was the color of the sheets
on the bed where she used to read
as the windows fogged
raindrops racing down
and tracing the lines she'd drawn with her fingers
of fleeting ideas and childish drawings.
she used to think she could stay there forever.

brown was the color of the eyes
that watched as people walked by each day
and her naivety was a sort of haven.

gone is the time she spent playing
with cabbage-patch dolls on her bed,
the desk is starting to get a little bit dusty, but
her mind still remembers the times she waited up
until midnight
and her walls still remember the endless laughter.

white is the color of the shelves that line her walls
but they're empty and forlorn now,
their items in a suitcase, packed away.

purple is the color of her mind
and the chaos
it's real and they swear it's there
warning her to stay in this bubble.

to leave her here would be cruel,
her downfall,
her end.

to leave her here would be generous,
her salvation,
her dream.

mahika ray goswami

my window's like a graveyard

the stars don't shine on the water anymore
and i can't see you from my bedroom
does wishing upon stars really work, anyway?

i can spot you a million miles away
usually, but not now
and i used to tell you to leave me signs
you must be out of signs
or maybe the sky is too crowded these days
too much light, too many satellites
and not enough room for ghosts.

you're there
when i feel like a sailor
desperately searching for the north star
and for direction
when the waters are rough.

i haven't seen you lately,
it must be because of the pollution
i've wished and wished and wished,
maybe i stopped knowing where to look.

but my curtains are up
the stars don't shine on the water anymore
and i still look for them every night.

breaking news

there's a sickness going around,
and i'm watching it consume all of my friends.
i've heard it's worse than the flu.
i was told it can't be cured.
the symptoms: speaking in the past tense,
wanting to fall into old photographs,
and yearning for home,
except home is really the memory of childhood
that still flickers in the deepest corners of your mind.
no one wants to call in sick,
but everyone knows the sickness is eating away at them.
we've all been coughing up childhood
with a tissue in our hands and dread clogging our lungs.
we remember the times we were drunk on so many dreams
with no idea about how to achieve them.
we take wrong turns in hopes that we will lose ourselves to the past.
the sickness is in my bones.
i feel it in my throat.
i feel it in my icy hands that close around something
that was never meant to be held onto.

seasick, and still

sometimes i'm scared of water
when i can't hold it still,

but there always is
the kind of comfort that the sea brings to a sailor
and i'll stay when i'm seasick on the deck
from the unstable waters
i'll be there when it's smooth sailing,
i'll be there.

the wind will whisper in my ear
about you, so i know i'll be fine
i'll let you carry me with you
to where the ocean never ends.

i forgot what solid ground feels like
the wind has been so quiet lately
and the salt air is making my skin sting
as time passes, i forget less
can you come back now?

sometimes i get scared of memory
because time slips like water.

groundhog

i've been late to everything lately
including my own life.
i used to be a good racer
i ran fast enough that i looped around the track
but suddenly
i find that i'm trailing behind the versions of everyone else i used to pass by
and it's not a race
but i miss the sweet feeling of winning
and the hope of 'one day,'
slowing down every time i wonder
if i can even run towards that anymore.

every year
people stare at a hole in the grass
waiting for an animal to tell them what to do.
the groundhog was supposed to emerge
but it's behind schedule,
so they're disappointed.

i'm looking for a sign.
i don't *want* everything to be broken
but there needs to be a reason why
it all feels like it doesn't work
right?

a few days later and the groundhog surfaced
and people cheered
but then it saw its own shadow.

it wasn't time, yet.

still, there was hope.

and all the while
i'm staring at the back of someone else's blurry head
running, still
and wondering if that could have been me
if i wasn't chased by doubt.
my life keeps feeling
like someone else's metaphor,
like i'm a symbol in someone else's story.
it's a lesson.

now the lights are on

every day, someone you used to know
wakes up like it's okay to not know you anymore
they eat breakfast and
they leave dishes in the sink and
they forget your birthday
like it's an accident
and you do it too
when you rewrite timelines,
and fold away versions of yourself
into drawers you never open again
but then a song plays
or someone laughs a certain way
or the wind hits your face and it's too sharp against your skin
and just like that,
you're back inside something
you didn't know you still carried
and you look around dazed
like the power came back on
after a long storm
and everything looks familiar
but nothing is where you left it.

milk teeth

there are things i should've let fall out a long time ago
beliefs that sit in my mouth like milk teeth
that are loose and aching.

and still,
i never pull them
too scared of the pain,
and too stubborn to admit when i've outgrown something.

i keep biting down on old stories
and empty apologies
and on what used to fit but just doesn't anymore.

i don't know what's underneath,
but i know it's sharper.
bone, probably.
truth, maybe.

either way
it's coming.

Part II: Displacement

But time moves anyway. Displacement is the act of being moved without being asked and without warning. It's being plucked from what you know and dropped into something unfamiliar. It's a reshaping of the self that comes not by choice, but by force.

unfamiliarity

all too quickly
too many things started to change.
i saw the first white snowflakes fall on my skin
and could confirm that, yes,
they did have a pattern.
the streets are new, gray, a shock
because i am used to colourful shops
and worn-down houses and street dogs,
but it's *new*.
this is the new forever
walking around on a tidy street
with organized roads and fewer stores
and the brick buildings, all lined up and square,
not pink and blue and coloured with the rainbow,
and the city is a grid, not a maze,
and i'd like to stay here forever but
i'm dying to go home.
everything is poles apart
and this city is charged with uncertainty
and when i go back, everything back home has changed too,
where it should be the same, it's unfamiliar and new, but
i look up, and i find that the sky is still the same,
and the sun is still the same,
and my room is still the same,
and i am the only one that changed.

'american'

'american'
the word is on my tongue, a question
but it did not belong to me
in the way it belonged to others.
or, rather,
i rejected it-
didn't want it.
if it has to be one or the other,
as is expected,
'american' was not the word i chose.
i still didn't choose it when suddenly
and very unfairly
it latched onto me.
'american' belonged to me, suddenly
and i belonged to it, unfairly.

the in-between world

i don't feel that i am of india, america,
or anywhere.
what can i call the in-between world where
with every step i take on american soil it seeps into my accent
my skin
my personality
my everything?
the in-between world where
the second i return home,
america is inevitable
a looming cloud above my head
and ready to burst with rain,
which washes my skin clean but weighs me down,
the in-between world where my two selves are sown up
to meet in the middle,
but never one?
never can be?
never wants to?

summer fruits

the mornings turn warmer
and the trees lean gently towards the source,
not sun-drunk yet, but tasting it.
i bite into a plum;
it's the first of the summer fruits.
i drizzle chocolate on strawberries
each one a red flare of warmth
that disappears too fast.

what is it about summer fruits
that makes them sweeter than the rest?
is it how they come
all at once
demanding to be tried,
then vanish before you're ready,
or how they rot too quickly
before enough time has passed?
is it how you miss them before they're even gone?
is it that they stay sweeter in memory
because they're gone?
and what is it about this?
how it's addicting
like a handful of blueberries,
where i don't know if one's sweet, another sour,
where one's soft, another cold.
like with my mangoes,
there's a pit in my stomach,
a hollow i try to eat my way around.

and the pit left behind
is the only reason i know
that there was once anything sweet around it
at all.

i reach for the last nectarines,
but soon that turns into reaching for red apples.
i bite into them
wondering if it counts as feeling full
if i still miss the transience of my summer fruits.

in the fall, i dream of bursting figs
and raspberries warmed by sun,
while holding a bowl of autumn fruits
that i used to fill with farmer's market berries,
some sour, some not,
but i only remember the sweetest ones.

pressed flowers

what is *forever*
if not a promise made to pacify you
for the time being?

sheer willpower wouldn't keep you here
neither could me giving it my all
so i'm familiarizing myself with the the truth:
things can die early.

the flowers are picked as buds
the colours could have been so beautiful
once they bloomed
but it was too early and the petals hadn't opened
and now, instead
we're pried open
then trapped between pages,
pressed flat by the weight of time
pressed into the world forever
in memory, at least
sealed like a case, not to be reopened.

it is beautiful because i know these colors
but they're not soft, anymore
nor lively
and long gone.

but sometimes, the imprint of light stays on your eyelids
long after you've closed them
as a punishment for looking into the sun
and looking too long at something you couldn't keep.

forever isn't real, you know.

olive branch

it is a sunny day
warm enough that the heat burns my scalp
i sit clutching the line
the hook has been bobbing on the water.
i'm wondering if the fish will ever bite
but it circles
waiting.

on my bed, i played a guessing game with myself
i bet you'd call me in a few days
when you'd thought everything over, maybe
i circled
waiting.

what would i do if i was a fish
and i had to swim around
and couldn't rest my fins all day?

do fish have existential crises?

it's tiring to swim in circles
i think waiting is overrated.
the fish was smarter
it didn't bite
and i wonder
distantly
if i used the wrong bait.

luck, if you're listening

under the lampshade
i'm holding my eyelash up to my face
on the tip of my finger and blowing
then pretending i don't see it landing on the table three feet away.

pretending i believe in signs
like a ladybug on a chain around my neck.

luck, if you're listening,
i'd say now is the time.

i've been searching since i was a kid but
the four leaf clover hasn't turned up yet
though the grass keeps growing every year
and the sun hasn't given up,
and somewhere, someone's probably finding
exactly what i've been looking for.

maybe, then, the next eyelash will work
or maybe it'll be the one after that.

pictures as evidence

i bought a camera
because i thought time couldn't steal memories from me,
if they lived somewhere that wasn't in my head.
i thought
it was foolproof.

you were in the frame of my photos,
not as the center,
but in the landscape.
my eye's lenses
and the camera's
refocused the frame
fixing on you, anyway.
our cameras shuttered and
i was in a few of your photos
and you were in mine.
which is to say that i have pictures as evidence
that we were good, once.
which is to say that i'm not actually sure
if it was doomed the whole time,
but i wonder if you knew
like i wonder if the candids i caught of you
were posed for.

when a picture felt like the last one
i'd take of you
i watched your camera shutter
a final time

and i had to turn mine off,
the pictures coming out all blurry without a focus,
aghast with the knowledge
that my knowing you was hindered
like a dam was built
to reshape the landscape
of my ever-flowing river of
infinite knowledge of you
that i had molded myself.
and i have snapshots of you
over years,
and you of me,
yet we will never trade pictures again.

the camera, apparently,
can make some memories sour like milk
while my mind serves as a freezer.
and now,
when your camera shutters,
i am nowhere near it.

a ghost's appetite

if i see you again one day
will you feed my hunger?

will you say hello,
then apologize for starving me?
for leaving me in silence
to gnaw on the spaces where words should have been?
or will you walk by
treating me like the ghost i became
where my bones are hollowed out
by what craving left behind?

there is hunger here, but not in my belly.
it's behind my teeth
in the space where words rot,
where i never got to say
please don't go.
where i never got to say
i would've been there
if you had asked.

i'll stay on the deck
a stray, always lurking
in the amber of your porch light
waiting to be fed.

and after the famine
finally swallows me whole
what if you just can't see me
at all?

citrus stains

someone said lemon water helps
with digestion or vitamin c or mornings.
i can't tell if it's working
but the sting of citrus feels honest
and i've been craving honesty lately.

sometimes i light candles i won't pray by and
i put on face masks like they can soothe
something deeper than skin
and every ritual is a quiet war
i spill juice
then i clean the counter three times.

is regret a stain or
something you can scrub out
if you try hard enough?

Part III: Resonance

After the disruption, there's the reflection. Resonance is the vibration, the inward ringing after the outward shift. It's the memories buzzing in the walls of new rooms and the sound of the past and present meeting. This is when memories return not to haunt, but to teach.

mirror, mirror

i know you got everything you wanted.
you wear my dreams so easily like they were always yours,
but they were mine, too,
sitting heavy in my palms and too much for me to hold.
you never learned what it's like to have nothing to say
you spoke every word i swallowed
because i grew to find too much safety in silence.
for everything i feel proud of myself for,
you already had it, easy,
and that's not to say you didn't work hard
only that you never had to fight just to start.
you're the one who'll make my younger self proud.
you're the one who'll make it.
i'll tell myself i hate you for that,
that i want you to also feel the weight
of everything i could have done better,
but you're everything i wanted to be.
it breaks my heart to think about the potential i had
and you, the only one who knew what to do with all of it.

fixer

my fingers are made of glue,
aching from being stuck to things i shouldn't have touched.
everything looks like it could use help.
i could use my sticky fingers to fix the cupboard
and the television
and the cracked kitchen chairs.
maybe they could fix home and everything in it
and everyone in it.
perhaps they'd hold themselves together at last.

but i don't know what's wrong
because they keep getting stuck to everything now,
clinging unhelpfully.
they aren't gentle anymore.
sometimes too much of the surface rips off
pushing splinters into my skin
not the fixer
in fact, probably the mess.

existentialism

the phrase 'in the grand scheme of things'
settles like a cold shadow in my head
and just over there is a woman
who views life differently
and wouldn't for a second entertain the haze of my rose-tinted glasses
but i watch her walk up to a stranger
soon they're talking like old friends
and i itch to know what that feels like
what wearing someone else's mind would feel like.

i sometimes wonder
how the earth doesn't collapse in on itself
with how important it is
or how unimportant
and how big the souls of strangers must be
and just how many there are
and how we will never know each other
though we may cross paths
and, still, how we do know each other
in some ways that matter.

i wonder whose souls i have known previously
before we made it here
only to now be fated to cross by one another
on a street
once.

maybe it's enough to live this way
in wonderment
for better or for worse
for as long as we all shall live.

in spirit

you hear things crashing to the floor,
lightning strikes and thunder roars,
you see him crumpled on the ground,
a world is shattered, an ache profound.

the tumor is benign, you turn to rejoice,
you finally find your hopeful voice,
you seize the second chance at life,
feeling your spirit on an upward rise.

it's back again; that empty feeling,
the days start blurring, your head is reeling,
"there's nothing we can do," they said,
"take me back home, to my own bed."

your pillar is gone, they say he's dead,
something you can't reconcile in your head.
in a room of people, when he's not there,
you're okay, you can feel him everywhere.

growing pains

the realization was like a bucket of ice water.
i miss ignorance,
but it's gone
like the dryness of my clothes when the water fell.

apparently, the shivering comes with adulthood.
apparently, there's no fire that can calm it.
there are more growing pains as inches of truth appear in my bones.
there's the crack of my ribs under pressure
and i think that if only i'd kept my eyes and ears closed
there wouldn't be so many.

what i mean is the truth has been a lot.
i think it must be a liar
otherwise it means i'm wrong, and we both know i'm not.

what i mean is childhood has left with its blindfold,
but i'm still convinced it's shoved away
on the top shelf of my cupboard from when i was told to clean my room.

i was a messy child. well, *am*.
it cost me the blindfold, but i really wish it didn't.
and what i really mean
is that i always try to hold onto everything
but it's not like i was given more than two hands,
so i'm realizing i was bound to lose.

what i mean is it was fated.
i knew what was coming, just not *how*.
the *how* would have helped.
the *how* was the armor.
i missed out on the armor,
yet i wanted to fight?

i'm going to stand still
and wait for the blow while the secrets that only children know leave me.
it's scary to forget what matters and what the whole point is.
what i mean is adulthood is kind of too close to me right now and
i need space .
what i mean is...

i lost my train of thought.

between you and i,

there are petty arguments
in place of understanding
we always ask each other
if the other is listening to know or to reply
but when i fight with you
every time i speak it's a one-woman show
my fault, i take the bait
and my gosh
this is not the script from my head
we fight, then
i am gearing up to leave
when you, as though nothing went wrong,
order my favorite dessert like a memorized script
in a second i'm left questioning
everything
because i'd spent weeks with the knowledge
that you just don't know me at all
was i wrong?

give me a reason, and i'll throw you a bone

and i feel a little bit bad about it
mostly, i just want to see if you can chase
like i do, like i used to
and you taught me to play this way
i learned all the rules
as you threw out reasons like breadcrumbs
for me to follow
disguising it as affection
this is muscle memory now
when i toss out reasons to you
waiting to see if you will follow them
if you can even handle your own game
if you can chase without expecting mercy
if you can love anymore
despite the path of destruction
i'm bitter
i'm sorry
not enough, though
to make it easy.

snakes and suits

there are many ways you can approach the upcoming situation:
- you can do what i did and ghost (strongly advise against this)
- you can be a good friend
- you can stop being scared of everything.

the fear makes you like a corporation
you run on selling (synthetic & bad quality) goods
but why not use better material?
well, so what if the cost rides up?
find out what you're afraid of and
don't hiss before you know what's approaching you.

you're afraid of pain like a snakebite
it will either sting and be harmless
or sting and be fatal.
you're afraid of the fear of the sting
and paralyzed before the wound comes
so you can't even get past that to find out the next part.
so you'll never know what would have been harmless.

you can pick your poison
and wear the suit and run the corporation
or you can find out how snake bites sting.
you're gloriously unaware of (real) pain
and you can't try to make up a version if only to know what other people
feel like
because you're recreating it wrong.
you'll know a real sting when it comes.

flight risk

you push sweet lullabies into her ears
of running to the clear water
and to the dark, magical woods
and running back into your arms again,
always
running
too pure to be allowed to stay
eyes wide like a curious child
eyes wide like a soldier in line of fire.

when a bee lands on a baby's breath
and everything tilts on its axis
just a little bit
the world will shift
from faithful to wavering
then, she will be ready to go.

she wants to be orbiting
her planets closely
spinning
and ready, always ready
and never grounded.

there is a tether that no number of saws can snap
she asked to remain anchored
but she has to be a flight risk
just like you.

windcheater

there's a moment
when you can see the calm before it slips
it's in the way someone holds themselves a little too tight,
like they know something's about to come loose.

i watch it happen, slowly
how you crack beneath the surface first
then
you break
like a fever,
burning from the inside out
like a storm gathering
too quickly to hide from
and loud, because you want us to know.

you aren't sure how to reign it in, yet
but you try to calm the wind
so that maybe it could lift a kite
instead of tearing down the sky.
and it does,
until the kite catches on a branch and rips
though you hadn't meant to let it go that far,
so it's unclear if you're the wind or the break.

i forgive you because you're atlas holding up the sky,
though you're looking around for someone to take it from you,
and looking my way.

marionette

the touch
of your warm fingers pressed on my spine
pulling at the threads
that made my muscles twitch
it's instinct before intention
i'm ready to pull back already
even though i was prepared to stay like that
with you
forever
fighting against your motions
tugging on the strings
then letting them go
as though i was a puppet,
one hand pulling
the other loosening
you couldn't even decide
if you wanted me to dance
or to fall.

i romanticised the control you had
i thought i danced for love
and when you twisted,
so did i.

you should have picked, puppeteer
you can't call yourself something
and not follow through
you should have chosen
between puppeteering the strings forever
and never touching them at all.

because when you were gone
i was left
not dancing,
not falling,
limp
with my arms raised halfway
and my mouth opened for a line that wasn't going to come.

homage to my silence

this silence grows
reaching up;
a beanstalk above clouds.
this silence is big
and it takes up space
and it's uncharacteristically loud.
this silence stands desperately
still,
when it's coaxed and cajoled
and told to step aside and
my silence, it
drowns out chaos like
a riptide i create, and
it cries out
then calms down,
this silence
like the wilt of a rose;
prickling,
thriving,
tired,
but this silence,
with warmth
rivaling the brilliance of heaven
and fingers reaching out
to ask,
to help,
to go.
this silence holds a magnifying glass
at the details,
from the wings,

and this silence
is a tool,
a cutting-edge knife,
an advantage i have,
i keep.

quiet chaos

four times
 i hid
   the first because of fear
   the second due to panic
   the third because of stubbornness
   the fourth out of habit
four times
 i stood quiet
   watching people around me grow
   not allowing myself to take the risk
   in case of failure
   or in case i say the wrong thing
     i built up the confidence for ages
     only for it to fall apart when i needed it most
     i had to start again from the start
     with less motivation than i had before
   when the words tried to leave my mouth
   not even a whisper could be heard
   it was so quiet you could hear a pin drop
   yet my mind was blaring like a siren
  it was almost a force of habit
  when the words didn't come another time
  because i saw that nothing changed before
  and i thought if i don't say anything
  i don't upset or let anyone down
turning over a new leaf was not as easy as it sounded
i wanted what i thought was out of reach
but as soon as i walked those extra steps
i went further than i thought possible for me

new beginnings were meant to be hopeful
but all they left behind were a longing to go back
to what used to be rather than what is
and i had to find a reason
to make the change worth it
four times
        i spoke
                first because it wasn't a choice
                then because i wanted to change
                because of a surge of confidence
                and finally because i was afraid of starting again
        it feels like i'm myself
        but in a more confident skin
        and this skin i don't want to shed
        since it will allow me to do incredible things
now i'm determined
        to not let anything weigh me down
                not the fear
                        or the panic
                                or the stubbornness
                                or the habit.

Part IV: Momentum

Eventually, the stillness shatters. Momentum is the reclaiming of movement. It's stumbling, then striding. It's what happens after reflection, when you begin to adapt, to grow, and to move forward, though not always gracefully. This is not the end, but rather when you gain motion.

the world will move on

the cacti will grow flowers and
a desperately thirsty man will finally find water in the desert
it isn't a mirage like he thinks
rain will softly patter over a burnt field
so everything will seem right in this world
slightly better,
at the very least.

i never understood bittersweet
the bitter is so overwhelming
and the sweet is only a last-ditch hope
that tastes artificial on my tongue
so i said goodbye in just a bitter way,
to avoid this.

the world will heal
painstakingly, slowly,
we will move on
we'll all have epiphanies
and realize where it all went wrong.

after everything
our hands will be washed, cleaned, and wrung dry
and forever,
we'll have made the wrong choice.

heart-shaped strawberry earrings

it's summer now
hot enough that the heat burns my scalp
and it's been another year
of waiting out the cold
and now sunlight sneaks through the trees
once again,
melting my watermelon popsicle,
staining my lips red
(the months have also quickly passed us by,
but no one thinks about that
too hard).

i'm wearing heart-shaped strawberry earrings
from a closed drawer
like a child still exists from years ago
though the world insists
we must grow old.

they're red like love and
red like the fire ants
trailing up my arms
biting me,
forcing me to remember
the older we get,
the duller we are,
the more greedy and skeptical we are, and
how can anyone dimmed like that
fix the world?

i used to walk
and believe it was unmarked land
and treasure was real and
we were scavengers.

now i flinch
then shake the ants off
before i am able to bleed memory
because i grew to fear bugs
over the years,
so i forgot
what used to wake me.

the popsicle drips down my knuckles
like it always does in June,
sugar trailing in winding lines
while the rubber band
that used to catch the drip
at my wrist
is looped in my longer hair,
so it runs all the way down
to my fingertips,
where the ants come marching,
one by one
and i shake them off, afraid.

we are only doomed when we forget
how to be hopeful like we used to be
months or summers or decades ago.

hopeful like the girls
on the cracked sidewalk,
sweating beneath the fading sun

and making crowns
with ixora flowers
calling them 'flame of the woods'
and taking out the pistil
to taste the nectar
that is sticky like their promises.

but, if, instead of swatting the ants,
we swat the fear of discomfort,
they will be able
to bite us back
to wonder,
into a time when the golden hour
was a state of mind
and not just an hour.

fire ants trailing,
red like love and
red like my old heart-shaped strawberry earrings.

thump, thump, thump

the still-beating heart of calcutta
waits to resuscitate me.
each auto's horn translates,
honk, honk, honk
into *thump, thump, thump*.
the city's heartbeat, stitched to my own,
reminding me of a pulse
i thought i'd left behind.
reminding me
i still belong to its chest.

i reach my grandmother's house
after a long drive from the airport.
antsy because i'm home,
i ring the doorbell thrice
and it translates
ding, ding, ding
into *thump, thump, thump*.

immediately, i'm hit with mirth
and nostalgia
because the laughter bouncing off the walls
has shifted keys,
but it's familiar, all the same
and the furniture moved to new corners
but that couldn't erase our names
carved under desks
over years.

later, my grandmother has her hands clasped together
in prayer before the sun
and the first raindrops patter
on the windowsill on a muggy monsoon morning,
and it translates
tap, tap, tap
into *thump, thump, thump.*
i look out of the window
at the rain running into streaks,
slipping faster than my eyes can catch,
like memory itself resents me
for chasing what's ready to go.

and still,
for a few moments,
i am a child again,
steady
as if the rain paused
and i could cling on,
and i'm not constantly balancing two countries
like an uneven weighing scale.
it wasn't a fair competition, anyway
new york waits
for calcutta to let go.
adulthood waits, too,
for childhood to let go.

my family and i sit
hunched around a game of ludo
i roll a three and move my piece
and it translates,
clack, clack, clack
into *thump, thump, thump.*

when it's time to go,
and i'm on the plane,
i imagine my own heart
falling out of my chest
to lodge itself into calcutta's busy streets.
people secure their seatbelts on the plane
and it translates
click, click, click
into *thump...thump—*

and then the plane takes off.

my memory tries to resuscitate
the fading pulse
of a lively city
as i watch the lights grow smaller.
as i leave
the engine's hum drowns out
every beat
but
calcutta will wait
to resuscitate me.

spectacle

this is for the ones who cheered,
then asked why she couldn't stay balanced forever.

when she was a circus,
it was a one-woman show
with the world watching from the front row
waiting to see how far she could fall.
impressive, they'd say.
they loved the tightrope years best,
the breath they held
for the thrill of maybe watching her slip.
what a performance, they'd say.

she juggled apologies,
balanced between too much and too quiet,
smiling the whole while
with her mouth full of sharp, useless words.
she can't say anything
because perfection and womanhood are bound together
like twin stars.
when the show ends
she's sweeping the arena in silence,
trying to find all she dropped
in the mess of sequins and feathers.
everyone is long gone, now
but sometimes she still bows,
just in case the world is watching.

the compass

in another life, you are a pirate.
a captain.
the trouble that you cause is softened
by smile lines.
i watch you navigate chaos with a sharp eye
a skill you've extended to me
because you have many tools in your toolbelt
because the ocean is so unforgiving
that to come out of a storm unscathed
is a rare thing
and somehow, you have, many times before,
and unfortunately,
there are many storms to come
and such is life
but we will have faith, you and i,
with your loyal crew
steady as the stars you follow
running from your enemies towards,
you never say what, but
something more.
and so far, the constellations never steered us wrong
and i trust that you know this ocean
because you have mapped it out
out of sheer dedication
and maybe it was survival, too.
and i hope
that one day you will find enough treasure
to make up for the lifetime of storms
so you can let go of the wheel
and rest.

awed

awe is a dangerous thing
it stuns your senses
and, well, what can you do then?

i have never seen a deer in headlights
but i imagine it to be a gruesome scene.
innocence killed by awe
so incredibly original.

pain is a journey but
i've been looking for ways around it
every time i get close
there's that awe again,
sneaking up the knobs of my worn spine.

i'm always trying to save time, though
i'm not sure how valuable time is
if it hurts.

one way
to bypass pain, i thought,
is to try to inflict love upon every scratch,
hoping it works as a bandaid,
but i don't think love was meant
to stick to skin like that.

the awe in love leaves a bitter taste in my mouth
that i can never wash away,

so
when i run out of reasons
to sprint through the pain,
as always,
i'll end up walking across fields and along roads
of endless dandelions that i'll blow

and watch
with awe
as the petals fly away
with my only wish.

abhaya

some storms arrive quietly
without thunder or warning.
some storms arrive with a door left unlocked,
and a man deciding he can snuff out a light.

a girl grew up with plans
she learned the pulse of the human body and
moved through hallways under harsh lights
on aching feet, and offered herself
again and again
because that's what she was taught to do:
heal.

a woman
in a world that loves her in theory
but can't protect her in practice
was taken by someone who believed
his want was worth more than her life;
one moment that undid lifetimes of sacrifice.

power wins.

but there were candles on the street like stars plucked from the sky
flickering in the steady hands of the people
willing to carry her through the dark.

a woman does everything right,
and she becomes a girl with no name
in a protest,
and she still becomes a headline
and she still becomes a lesson.

and she's named *fearless* because that's what they hoped she was
when she died
even though she shouldn't have had to be
because it's easier to sleep at night
believing she faced it unafraid
than to live with the knowledge that a fearless girl was killed scared.

so, the name doesn't land as a tribute
but as a story they told each other
so they wouldn't have to carry the weight
of what the system let happen.

she became larger than loss
not a martyr, but a reminder
that when justice waits too long
people will carry it themselves.

their goal was to shut off the lights.
and, still, in the dim hours
when the night should have swallowed her name,
there were fires still burning.

the people will win,
just hold on.

for now

i'm really okay with you being gone.
i'm in my brick house looking out
and the air is heavier, probably with the dust
everywhere
because i haven't moved since you left
i haven't swept the floors or opened the windows, either
which is okay, for now.

but suddenly i really feel the ivy
twisting and growing over windows,
over doors
claiming what used to be open and bright.
how am i supposed to reach you, now
that the vines grew thick and tangled?
how do i find the keys to a door
that's been swallowed by age and time?
how am i supposed to leave, now
that the dust has almost settled?

and how am i going to convince myself, this time
that all of this is *just for now?*
that maybe someday i'll find a crack in the wall
that the vines forgot to wrap?
then, i'll feel a sliver of sunlight again
and step through.

acknowledgements

First of all, I want to thank my family for their unwavering support and love throughout this process. This would not be possible without them. Thank you to Ma and Daddy for sitting with me through every single draft.

I'm endlessly grateful to my friends for cheering me on through every stage of this, for listening, and for always believing in me.

I am so, so thankful to Sue Mashi for thoughtfully editing my poems and offering continuous encouragement and mentorship, and finally, to Bobo Mama (instagram: @bobocalcutta) for bringing the book to life with his beautiful artwork on the cover.

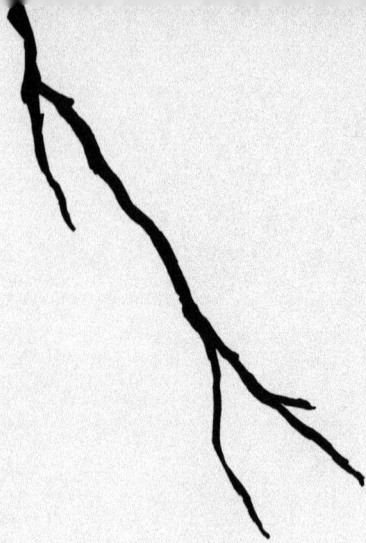